Wallace & Gromit

CURSE OF THE WERE-RABBIT

The Essential Guide

HOP 2 1T

Written by Glenn Dakin

Wallace & Gromit

Curse of the Were-Rabbit

The Essential Guide

PUNCH AND
JUDY TENT

LOW CALORIE,
CHEESELESS
SALAD

TOTTINGTON HALL
SNOW GLOBES

CHOPPING BOARD

TOY RABBIT
FAIRGROUND PRIZES

SCARECROW

MR CALICHE'S
GARDEN RAKE

CHEESES DISPLAY AT
THE COMPETITION

MRS WINDFALL'S
HANDBAG

GOLDEN CARROT PRIZE

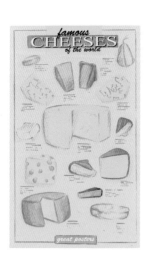

PAN RACK

MR MULCH'S
PIPE

CHEESE
POSTER

PULLY

MR CROCK'S HAT

MRS WINDFALL'S
HATPIN

MISS THRIPP'S
FALSE TEETH

KITCHEN
UTENSILS

Contents

VICTOR'S
ROSES

TOOL BOX

LAWNMOWER

WHEELBARROW

FAIRGROUND
GAME

OIL
PAINTING

Wallace

Inventor, cheese-fanatic and dog-lover, Wallace is a great British eccentric. He's the type of man who'd much rather spend weeks creating a machine to put his wellies on him than simply do it himself. Despite his love of new ideas he is old-fashioned at heart and adores his mug of tea, warm slippers and cream crackers – all provided by Gromit of course!

In case he gets peckish, Wallace keeps a secret stash of cheese under his hat.

- Slippers
- Breakfast
- Newspaper
- Walkies

Inventor

Wallace likes to live in a push-button world, where simple household tasks are turned into complicated and alarming mechanical processes. With him, even getting out of bed can be a high-tech, high-impact experience.

Wallace usually wears fashionable knitwear, but for rabbit-catching he wears a nibble-proof boiler suit.

New venture

Wallace's career as a pest-control expert began by chance when he developed the "pre-dug rabbit burrow" to divert bunnies away from his own garden.

Love and romance

While Wallace has been in love before (remember Wendolene?), no one has actually managed to tie him down and that's how Gromit would like to keep it. It's difficult enough for Gromit to keep his master's feet firmly on the ground! Now that the ravishing Lady Tottington is in his sights, will life ever be the same again?

Diet

Gromit has put his master on a cheese-free diet, but Wallace has ingenious places to hide his cheese. There's Parmesan in the salt and pepper pots, cheese slices in the CD cases and cheddar in his old socks!

Almost every morning Wallace's middle-aged spread gets him in a jam.

Wallace's inventions

• Wallace once built an extraordinary hamster-driven computer that was able to pinpoint exactly where the jam is in a doughnut and could also play dominoes to international standard. A very useful machine to have around!

• One of Wallace's cleverest inventions is the lightweight, portable bus stop, though using it guarantees that three buses will come along at once.

• His favourite invention is the everlasting cream cracker, perfect for eating with Wensleydale – again and again.

• Banned from toy shops, his noiseless whoopee cushion is silent but deadly.

Wallace's favourite magazine is filled with stories about celebrity horticulurists, and is the inspiration behind many of his gardening gadgets.

Man's best chum

Wallace and Gromit have a special understanding, based on Wallace threatening to put Gromit on a lead if he's bad. Their friendship is made of brains and hard work, with Gromit providing both.

Gromit

The most faithful dog anyone could wish for, Gromit serves his master loyally through thick and thin – usually thick ideas from Wallace and thin rewards for Gromit. This resourceful pooch has learnt to stay one step ahead of Wallace's potty plans and finds ways to put everything right in the end.

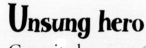

Unsung hero

Gromit slaves away in the shadows while his master gets to hobnob with local toffs. He is ever-reliable, whether he's bagging bunnies, riveting a monster-cage, operating a giant she-rabbit puppet or planning a sensible diet for Wallace to ignore.

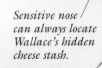

Sensitive nose can always locate Wallace's hidden cheese stash.

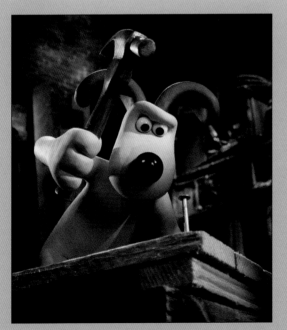

It's a dog's life!

A hundred rabbit hutches with waste systems don't make themselves, and Gromit's endless toil saves Anti-pesto from being knee-deep in rabbit droppings. If Gromit ever left, it would take several people to take over his roles as butler, welder, carpenter, chef, electrician and chauffeur!

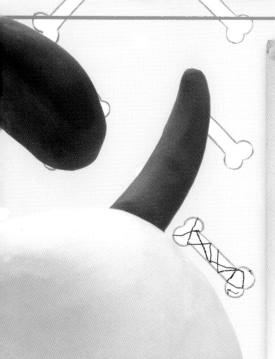

How to care for your marrow

Every day, without fail, Gromit measures the marrow to check that it is racing towards championship size. A picture of the Golden Carrot Prize trophy inspires him.

Gromit's secret is to add a boiled, smelly sock to his plant feed. Using a teapot with a watering can rose, he serves it up in style.

A bedtime hug reveals the affection between the dog and the marrow.

Lastly, Gromit covers his pride and joy with a warm and cosy electric blanket.

Doggy details

- After a hard day, Gromit likes to play music to relax. He often plays "Yelp!" by the Beatles.

- Gromit's favourite foods include bones and dog biscuits, but he's also partial to Dolly Mixtures!

- He's a real film fan and watches *Indiana Bones* at least once a week.

THE PLANT SUITE

Talented paws can do just about anything!

At Home

From the outside, 62 West Wallaby Street looks very much like any other British home. Inside, however, is a different story. Flashing lights and mechanical hands compete with tipping beds and the hundreds of rabbits who have taken up residence under the house in the basement.

Healthy living

Munchy brown flakes and a dollop of middle-age spread on toast are barred from breakfast time by a zealous Gromit, as he attempts to turn 62 West Wallaby Street into a fat-free environment.

This service hatch not only brings Wallace his grub, but it's also a handy mini-lift for Gromit who uses it to keep up his reputation of being everywhere at one time.

Food for thought

The awful truth stares up at Wallace from his plate as the hard-line new health regime gets under way. Wallace is now so tubby he gets stuck in the trap door in his bedroom. Although it's fun watching the mallet hammer his master through the hatch, Gromit knows it's now time to put his paw down.

False grin is an attempt to mask his dislike of the new diet

For Wallace, organic vegetables are not a patch on his beloved cheese.

Our Valued Clients

Mrs Hedges

Prof. Chalke

Mr Mulch

Mr Shovel

Mr Frond

Mrs Mulch

Mr Cloone

Mrs Spade

Mr Growbag

Mr Pippin

Miss Thrip

Lady Tottington

Mr Trowel

Mrs Green

Mrs Bird

Operations room

Displaying their valued clients in pictures over the mantelpiece is a vital part of Anti-pesto's rapid-response set-up. Vegetable vandalism is spotted by garden gnomes. Their alert signal flashes through the eyes of the victim's portrait, enabling the team to strike instantly!

Everyday lightbulbs adapted to make electric eyeballs

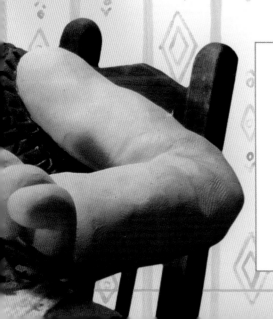

Home sweet home

• Wallace keeps his favourite books, *East of Edam* and *Grated Expectations*, on his bedside table.

• Extravagant wallpaper is ideal for Wallace as he thinks it makes him look interesting.

• Wallace bricked up the fireplace long ago, as Gromit had a puppy-hood fear of Father Christmas.

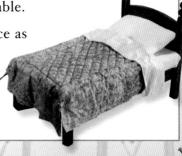

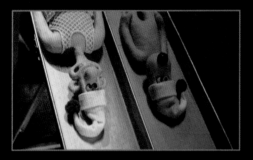

1. If an intruder is detected in a client's garden, Wallace is woken by an irresistible smell of cheese.

2. Gromit is prodded awake, then both his and Wallace's beds tilt, sending them down a chute.

3. The Anti-pesto agents are served tea while being tipped into their wellies. Their nightcaps are replaced with pest-control caps.

4. Somersaulted into his boiler suit, Wallace manages to avoid spilling a single drop of tea.

Anti-pesto Alert

Run, rabbits, run! When pest-control company Anti-pesto is called into action, no radish-rustler, lettuce-lifter or celery-swiper is safe! Legendary garden guardians, the fearless vegetable vigilantes are on standby day and night to put an end to naughty nibbling.

Cap – never worn back to front

100kg block of Yorkshire sandstone provides the pulling power to yank Wallace out of bed in the morning.

Boiler suit – perfect attire for boiling the kettle for a cuppa and clearing the town of pests.

Customer care cards

Customer satsifaction is of utmost importance to Anti-pesto. To ensure that their clients' gardens are kept safe from furry foes, Wallace fills in a personalized card for every customer. Each card contains details of Anti-pesto's protection plan and lists the precious vegetables under their care.

The gnome guard

This innocent-looking gnome is in fact a top state-of-the-art garden monitor. Motion-sensitive diodes in its eyes pick up the first sign of a hungry intruder and send an emergency radio signal back to the Anti-pesto nerve centre – Wallace's living room.

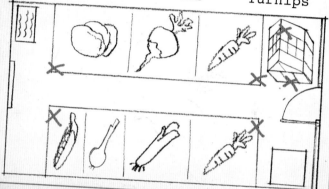

Customer Details

62 West Wallaby St.

Tel. 5421

 ANTI-PESTO S.W.A.T. TEAM

Mr Growbag
37 Plumton Way

Tel. 4667

Notes
Customer will flatten molehills. Don't squash globe artichokes.

Security Points	Vegetables	
2: Greenhouses	Carrots	Sprouts
4: Gnomes	Peas	Onions
	Leeks	Turnips

Sign of security

The official Anti-pesto sign is the ultimate symbol of garden safety. Potential pests who see this notice will know that they enter the garden at their own peril. Sadly, rabbits can't read.

Bunny-bagging techniques

Strong canvas sack prevents bunnies hopping

• Lure the suspect with Mr Browning's organic carrots – no bunny will be able to resist.

• The "pre-dug rabbit burrow" – an extendable tube that confuses bunnies into believing that it is one of their rabbit warrens. Manufactured by Tubes 'R' Us.

• Immobilize rabbit by popping a tough sack over its head. What it can't see, it can't eat.

• Lightning-fast rabbit-grabber can seize a bunny while avoiding any risk of being nibbled yourself.

Rabbit-grabber – causes no harm to detainee

The Bunvac 6000

The BV 6000 acts as a giant hoover and its suction power can clear a lawn clean of rabbits in seconds. Its nozzle is inserted into the ground and the bunnies are sucked up into a glass collection chamber.

The Bunvac is capable of 125 rpm – that's "rabbits per minute". But it's not bunny-specific and can suck up anything that gets in its way, including wayward wigs.

Anti-pesto slogan promises to dispose of pests humanely.

SAFE·SECURE·HUMANE
PEST CONTROL

Tel. 2143

ANTI-PESTO
S.W.A.T. TEAM

Tyres with extra thick tread – perfect for pursuing giant bunnies down rabbit holes

Logo designed by Gromit

HOP 2 IT

Tools of the Trade

Robust, trusty – and ever so slightly rusty – this souped-up pestmobile is ready to roar into action whenever the alarm is sounded. Don't let its ageing exterior fool you – it's packed to the hubcaps with Wallace's newest gadgets.

De-mudding device

The hidden De-mudding device can shake the van free of dirt, with all the energy of Gromit shaking off his weekly bathwater. This can be a useful extra, if, for instance, the van has strayed down a giant rabbit hole.

The self-cranking auto-start mechanism revs up the van's engine with its unique electronic hand system. In an emergency situation it can also be used to give hand signals or even pat angry dogs.

Grille slides up to release auto-start arm

Customized numberplate

The Competition

Lady Tottington's family has held a Giant Vegetable Competition for over 500 years. Anticipated with fanatical enthusiasm, it is considered, by the veggie-mad townsfolk, to be the event of the year, as they all strive to carry off that ultimate prize – the Golden Carrot.

PROTECTED BY ANTI-PESTO

Show time

The big event's spectacular array of sideshows reveal the population's second favourite pastime – bogus bunny bashing. The Bag-a-bunny shooting gallery gives them a chance to blast rabbit targets, and the popular Whack-a-bunny stall even lets little old ladies go mallet mad and pound the floppy-eared foe.

TOTTINGTON HALL
GIANT VEGETABLE COMPETITION
FUNFAIR! SIDESHOWS!
4 DAYS TO GO!

Ornamental Brassica – needs a lot of love

Historic Highlights

• In 1956 Mr Growbag grew a brussel sprout so big it came second in the cabbage competition.

• Wensleydale was excluded from the cheese contest for many years as it kept disappearing, despite Wallace guarding it.

• A turnip resembling an undisclosed member of royalty was banned from the competition in 1977 as it was disrespectful.

• In 1999 Victor Quartermaine's dog, Philip, was sent home because of an unwelcome last-minute entry in the homemade compost contest.

Posters promote vegetable fever, as they count down to the competition (something many townsfolk have trouble with).

The Golden Carrot

24 carat carrot

The most valuable root vegetable replica ever created, the Golden Carrot Prize is kept for one year by each winner of the Giant Vegetable Competition. A priceless work of art, it also makes a cracking weapon, should the need arise.

Hand-engraved by town goldsmith Phinias Pod.

GOLDEN CARROT

Who dares wins

Townsfolk will stop at nothing to gain an advantage in the vegetable competition: pumpkins get midnight pep-talks, music is played to peas and marathon coverage is shown to runner beans.

Great disasters

Fears that some terrible disaster will come along and ruin the competition are not all fantasy. In 1932 the Great Slug Blight caused cauliflower carnage and in 1955 many potential prize vegetables were cut down in their prime by the rapid runaway lawnmower.

Townsfolk

Howling, boggle-eyed and horrible to behold – no, that's not the Were-rabbit, it's the townsfolk, when they turn into a desperate mob. Fearing for the safety of the things they love most – their prize vegetables – these kind and gentle souls can change from humble garden-lovers into an hysterical horde, bent on revenge and destruction!

Helmet hides an unusual dome-shaped head

Extremely bushy moustache hides a cynical sneer

PC Mackintosh

PC Mackintosh is the only man in town who has no time for vegetables, and that's because they make his life a misery. Endlessly plodding his beat to protect beetroot, peas and caulies, PC Mackintosh is long overdue a holiday. Unfortunately, he won't get one until the day of the great competition is over!

Being the voice of reason, PC Mackintosh believes there is a perfectly logical explanation for the vegetable vandalism plaguing the town. The perpetrator must be a jealous gardener – who else could it be?

Traditional Truncheon – the Thief-Thrasher Mk II

Notebook – PC Mackintosh is never without his notebook to record details of crimes (although it's mostly used to write down his shopping list).

Traditional Irish Brogues – the official shoe for a Plod to plod in.

Community spirit

In a small town, people care about each other's problems – especially when that problem is a 10-foot-high beast! The crisis brings folk together, just like after the spade and hoe shortage between '41 and '45.

Mr Crock

Bushy-bearded Mr Crock does not have much luck as far as vegetables are concerned. He used to run a mushroom farm until it burnt down, leaving him with far too much room on his hands. For the last 12 years he has consistently come second in the Giant Vegetable Competition, frustratingly always one step away from the Golden Carrot prize.

Pea-green hat

Miss Thrip

This sour-faced old spinster is a hardliner in the town mob and is prepared to throttle the local police to get justice. Any sign that she has wasted her money on inadequate vegetable security measures drives her into a frenzy.

In times of peace and happiness, Miss Thrip is another person entirely. She becomes so quiet and retiring that she even has a green handbag, scarf and hat to blend in with her runner beans.

Mushy-pea-green handbag

The Locals

Every town has its charming, delightful, kind-hearted old dears that love to spread a little sunshine around and this one is no exception. But, if you dare to cross their vegetable patches, you may see a different side to them! These lettuce-lovers are highly competitive – a fact that becomes clearer as the contest draws near.

Every year the Giant Vegetable Competition turns even the most normal of townsfolk into vegetable-obsessed oddballs!

Untamable hair escapes from headscarf

Mr Mulch's poor ears have taken a battering over the years due to his wife's constant nagging.

Mr & Mrs Mulch

Mrs Mulch loves her prize pumpkin so much she refers to it as her baby and pushes it around in a pram. Dutiful Mr Mulch has no choice but to go along with his wife's every whim. Sadly, there is to be no happy Halloween for this pumpkin, as it meets a nightmare ending worthy of any horror film.

After the Were-rabbit's veg ravaging rampage, Mrs Mulch decares, "It's payback time!" She has plans for the Were-rabbit, and they don't involve tickling its ears!

Mrs Girdling

Hard-as-nails Gloria Girdling is famous for her "salt-first-ask-questions-later" approach to slugs. She still has a soft heart and each evening coos "nighty-night" to her lettuces.

Baggy stockings from kneeling to tend to vegetables

Unlike some townsfolk who trust Anti-pesto completely, Mrs Girdling takes no chances and secures her greenhouse with more locks than the Bank of England.

Left knee is prone to stiffness, especially after gardening.

Mr Growbag

Every town needs a doomsayer, and old Gabriel Growbag does his best to spread fear and dismay wherever he goes. The avid gardener is no stranger to misfortune. In 1949 he failed to attend the Vegetable Competition when, on his way there, hundreds of ducks flew overhead and pelted him with droppings. Now, if someone says "duck", he literally ducks!

Growbag was also a victim of the Great Slug Blight of '32, although some claim that he's not a reliable witness to its horror. Were the slugs really as big as pigs or had he been drinking too much of his own famous lupin wine?

Soil-encrusted gardening shoes

Tottington Hall

This monumental mansion has been the home of the Tottington family for centuries. With its vast gardens, Tottington Hall attracts many visitors during the Giant Vegetable Competition – mainly an endless stream of fluffy, salad-scoffing pests, to whom the vegetable patches are bunny paradise!

A haven of tranquillity for 364 days a year, the hall is a scene of hysteria for the other one – the day of the competition.

A lawn covered with hungry bunnies is enough to drive Lady Tottington hopping mad.

A temple to Mother Nature

Built by mistake on the ancient Lord Tottington's favourite vegetable patch, the great hall has been a shrine to root and fruit ever since – decorated with golden gooseberry leaves and plaster grapevines throughout. The Quartermaine family have long sought to marry into the property and have it gutted.

Imitation silk drapes – Lady Tottington is a campaigner for silkworm rights

Ornamental gooseberry leaves adorn each pillar

Grapevine moulding

Lady Tottington's stunning rooftop conservatory

Windows of the well-stocked Legume Library

Gromit ready for quick getaway if rabbits turn nasty

Food-fixated expression found on rabbit faces

Daisy chains are the last thing on this bunny's mind

ANTI-PESTO S.W.A.T. TEAM

The battle of the bunnies

It was a scene that would go down in Tottington Hall history forever. Anti-pesto took on the rabbit plague single-handed (and single-pawed) and won – without hurting even one of their furry foes. Anti-pesto's humane techniques ensure that everyone is a happy bunny!

Tottington Hall facts

• Designed in 1732 by architect Sir Christopher Wradish.

• Haunted by Greenfingers the Gardener, who was buried alive in the compost bin.

• During the competition, visitors can view the prune collection.

Lady Tottington

Animal-lover, vegetable-fancier and friend of fruit, Lady Campanula Tottington worships Mother Nature. She is kind to all earth's creatures, big and small. She even has a place in her heart for the pesky pests that ravage her gardens. She is a good soul, delightful and compassionate, with a hairstyle that's a cut above the rest!

Hair held in place by organic tree-sap hair gel

Trademark elegant pose

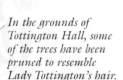

In the grounds of Tottington Hall, some of the trees have been pruned to resemble Lady Tottington's hair.

An English rose

Pictured here by her prize-winning lawns (until the bunny-invasion turned them into a battlefield), Campanula certainly has a striking appearance. She inherited her extreme looks from her ancestors, dating back hundreds of years.

Outfits

The talented aristocrat designs all her own dresses and accessories. At garden parties, her floral gowns, especially her famous daisy outfit, have attracted a lot of attention. A swarm of bees once pursued her into the garden lake where she had to hide for several hours until the swarm dispersed.

Wallace thinks Campanula looks smashing, whatever she is wearing.

The fashionable fabrics are made using only natural vegetable dyes.

Family tree

The Tottington family can date its noble origins back as far as the time of William the Conqueror, when they were among the first to be conquered. Well, it is hard to hide from invaders when you have bright-red hair that grows horizontally! The Tottingtons have not always loved vegetables. The Duke of Tottington was injured by a turnip in the marrow mutiny of 1846.

The first Lady Tottington may have invented this haircut to hide her pair of ridiculously large ears.

The Tottingtons have refused to change their telephones since they were installed between the wars. They have also kept the medieval boar-tusk toilet-roll holders.

One's facts

• Lady Tottington thinks that picking apples is cruel, and will only eat fruit that has fallen from free-range trees.

• She hates all types of blood sport and holds an annual "foxglove hunt" to replace the sport of fox-hunting. Nobody attends.

• Eating cheese is something that "grates" on Lady Tottington. This is bad news for Wallace!

Will Cupid strike for Campanula and Wallace?

Tea for two

The relationship between Campanula and Wallace is blossoming like the flowers in her conservatory. Wallace is swept off his feet by Lady Tottington's charms, but can he learn to love vegetables more than cheese?

The Conservatory

Lady Tottington's pride and joy is this veritable vegetable wonderland built on her rooftop. More than just a glorified greenhouse, it is her inner sanctum where she goes to commune with nature. Victor has never shown interest in Campanula's produce, but she has high hopes that Wallace will share her passion.

Grapes are only picked when the plant therapist says they are emotionally ready.

Stairway to heaven

A private lift takes her ladyship and any privileged guests up to plant paradise. She calls it her "Jacob's Ladder" as it takes her all the way up to heaven. The tiny elevator is a snug fit, but love-struck Wallace doesn't seem to mind!

Green finger facts

• The conservatory has a microclimate similar to a tropical island so Lady Tottington can produce exotic fruit and vegetables.

• The sprinkler system can simulate any natural rain effect, from a tropical monsoon to a November drizzle in Scarborough.

• No expense is spared when it comes to Lady Tottington's gardens. Only the best fertilisers are used to nourish her plants, including pricey peacock manure.

Tendril chair cost £5,000 at Chelsea Flower Show.

In her leaf-patterned dress Lady Tottington feels at one with her plants.

Paradise lost

Victor is the serpent in Lady Tottington's Eden. Once he gets hold of Tottington Hall, he plans to convert the conservatory into a rooftop squirrel-shooting facility – and bar. Wallace appears to be much more appreciative of Lady Tottington's paradise. In fact, he seems to be showing a little too much interest. Luckily Gromit is lurking in the undergrowth to prevent the veg from driving rabbit-brained Wallace into a feeding frenzy. As a last resort, Gromit makes use of the conservatory's sprinkler system to dampen Wallace's vegetable desires.

The crowning jewel in Lady Tottington's collection is the "Carotte d'Chantenay". This monster carrot could have a monstrous effect on Wallace, as it's succulent flesh may just bring the beast out in him!

Victor Quartermaine

Rotter, rascal and rabbit-hater, this upper-class cad is out to marry Lady Tottington so he can get his hands on her cash. The utter bounder has one secret – he is completely bald, and his terrible toupee often leaves him exposed at a crucial moment.

Horrific hairpiece – Victor believes this tall toupee makes him look distinguished.

Arrogant sneer

Traditional cad's cravat

Safari suit bought on his last hunting holiday

Cheapskate Victor shamlessly carries a pair of secateurs in his pocket so he can snip roses from Tottington Hall and give them to Lady Tottington as a bouquet.

Pockets used to store amunition for his guns

Natural born killer

Victor loves the sights of nature, especially when he's got nature in his sights! This heartless hunter will take a pot-shot at anything that moves, even if it's human, and especially if it's that Anti-pesto pest, Wallace.

Victor was an annoying brat as a child. When he was old enough, his father bought him this gun in the hope that becoming a huntsman would keep Victor out of the house.

Tough riding boots – good for stepping on caterpillars and other insects

Victor the hero

When the simple townsfolk believe Victor has killed the Were-rabbit and saved their competition, he enjoys the unlikely role of hero for once. But life isn't always easy for a legend, and Victor is quickly mobbed by the crowd who want him to touch their vegetables for luck! Victor's hero status proves to be very temporary and his true nature is soon revealed.

Pompous pose

Victor has spent years reeling in the bunny-loving Lady Tottington, and won't give her up to Wallace without a fight. When he sees Wallace with Lady Tottington, he stomps on her roses – and Philip follows suit.

Victor's blunders

• When Lady Tottington says she thoroughly disapproves of thoughtless killing, Victor replies that he thinks about killing a lot. This is a big mistake!

• Victor upsets the locals by telling them their produce is only good as bait.

• Let's face it – if vegetables had legs he'd shoot them!

Bunny-scaring snarl

Philip

In many ways Victor's dog, Philip, is very similar to Gromit – he's loyal, fearless, and utterly devoted to his master. But that's where the similarity ends. Philip can be sneaky and spiteful and always on the lookout for mischief.

The Cellar

Number 62 may look like any other house in West Wallaby Street, but underneath it lurks Anti-pesto's dark secret – a network of specially designed chambers for holding captured rabbits. Their basement has become a bunny bed and breakfast where the "guests" are well looked after by Gromit while Wallace tries to come up with a plan on what to do with the multiplying carrot-munchers!

Wallace's workshop

Away from prying eyes, Wallace also uses the cellar to work on new inventions. He doesn't like to be thought of as a "mad inventor", so he works on really sensible ideas, like his pocket lawn mower.

Feeding the masses

Every day the hopping hordes receive nutritious square meals (well round ones) of sliced carrot. A series of chutes in the kitchen go straight down into the cellar, and the healthy meals are supplemented by any veg that Wallace sneakily chucks down there from his own plate!

Safekeeping

The rabbits that Anti-pesto catch are housed in individual traditional rabbit hutches where they can be kept out of mischief until Wallace decides what to do with them!

Rabbit recycling

• Wallace has used the power generated by the constant rabbit-gnawing to transmit vibrations up to the roof and shake off birds that try to perch on his TV aerial.

• Rabbit droppings are compacted into compost cakes, sold through Mr Caliche's garden supplies business and "fed" as a Sunday treat to the town's spoilt vegetables.

• Carrot tops are squashed into a green slime that is no use. But if you hate carrots, it's fun doing the squashing!

Safety visor is recommended for construction work

This is the view from inside Hutch's hutch the morning after the Were-rabbit's first rampage. Can that sweet little fluffball really be the culprit?

Gromit adopts safety stance

Super hutch

This reinforced steel cage has been created by Gromit to hold the beast captive. Of course, it only works if you've put the right suspect in it.

Rivet gun bought from an advert in The Morning Post.

Mind-o-matic

Brain alteration is a harmless pastime, according to Wallace, and his Mind-o-matic could be a real boon to mankind. Originally designed to help Wallace overcome his love of cheese and go on a diet, it is soon given a more ambitious purpose – to alter the veg-ravaging habits of hungry bunnies!

Warning lights flash on and off to alert the operator that the Mind-o-matic is almost overloaded.

"Veg bad!"

Linking the Mind-o-matic to the Bunvac gives Wallace the chance to control the rabbits' minds and brainwash them into hating vegetables. Wallace accidentally kicks the switch onto "Blow" and a rabbit gets sucked into the mind helmet.

Lunar panels absorb rays from the full moon and transfer them into the helmet to boost the power.

Control panel is built into hand rest. Lunar panels are activated when the lever is pulled.

Gromit can't look as the bunny's brainwaves merge with Wallace's. The consequences are too dreadful to contemplate! At least it is safe to return the reformed, lettuce-loathing rabbits to the wild without fear of them re-offending.

The Morning Post and Ay-Up! for Wallace to read while under the helmet

32

Glass thought-control chamber is jumbo-sized for Wallace's enormous brainpower.

The Bunvac is connected and ready for thought transfer – provided it is used correctly.

This lever switches the Bunvac from suck to blow – disastrous if kicked accidentally.

Hutch

During the mind alteration experiment, a rabbit called Hutch exchanged brainwaves with Wallace. Hutch can now speak, walk upright and has taken to wearing tank tops. The reconstructed rabbit goes from carrot connoisseur to cheese expert, and proves that when it comes to swapping brains, he got the better deal!

Hutch's buck-toothed brethren can only gaze in wonder as he becomes the first rabbit to hop up the evolutionary ladder.

Rabbit replacement

Wallace, his brain reduced to a rabbity mush, looks on helplessly as a bunny steps into his slippers and takes over his life! Other than the fact that Hutch is slightly cuter, it's almost impossible to tell them apart!

The great bunny menace

They may look innocent, but as Wallace points out, rabbits are the ultimate vegetable-destroying machine! They have no hobbies outside of looking for food and eating it, which makes them a high-performance pest.

Bunnies also enjoy having more rabbits, and a mother bunny can have babies five times a year! That's a lot of hungry hoppers to feed!

— *This stomach is full of illegally obtained veg.*

Warren peace

Wallace's plan to rehabilitate rabbits, turning them into non-nibblers who we can share the countryside with, is a noble one. Victor Quartermaine would prefer to send them to "bunny heaven".

You've made your bed...

Having created a rabbit alter-ego for himself, Wallace has to look on the bright side. At least Hutch can help run Anti-pesto while Wallace goes into a fluffy-tailed frenzy.

Hutch cheekily adopts Wallace's favourite mug and makes it his own.

Huge ears can detect the rustle of a cheese pack from afar.

Rabbit nose, grown to human size, easily locates Wallace's hidden cheese.

Wallace's favourite tank top is a little large for Hutch.

Wallace's concealed crackers are also sniffed out.

Comfy slippers hide frighteningly large rabbit feet

Hutch vs Wallace

• Hutch eats more cheese than even Wallace would!

• The bunny fixes the Mind-o-matic, while Wallace goes bunny-brain bonkers.

• Hutch rescues Wallace in the van, despite no rabbit ever having driven before.

Rev. Hedges

Hair has receded backwards – and upwards.

This devout man believes in being kind to all God's creatures. However, if they try to invade his vegetable garden then he's quite happy to hand out advice on how to destroy the pests! His job is to watch lovingly over the simple folk of his parish, although some say he prefers to keep an eye on his beloved vegetables, especially the carrots.

Bags under his eyes caused by secret late night sermons at his allotment

"Bless you, Anti-pesto!" The vicar supports Wallace and Gromit's work in protecting innocent vegetables from sinful slugs.

Cassock covers a multitude of shins.

The Good Book

Hedges has rather unusual tastes for a man of the cloth, and is secretly a reader of *The Observer Book of Monsters*, which reveals such unholy terrors as the Were-cow, Brockula the vampire badger and Codzilla the demon fish.

Despite his loyalty to his library, Hedges can be guaranteed to be at the front of any goings-on in the town. It's a shame that no one can see past his hair!

Favourite hymns

- "Lettuce Praise Him" is ideal for singing in the greenhouse and encourages plants to grow cheerfully.
- "Cucumber My Lord" is quite encouraging for cucumbers that have been attacked by insects and are full of holes.
- "Marrow has Broken" is a bit of a no-no as it can make marrows depressed.

Church's best holy water sprinkler ensures all vegetables are covered evenly

Water is blessed before use.

Divine intervention

Is it cheating to sprinkle holy water over your plants? Not if nobody sees you, reckons the reverend, so he performs this service late at night, after evensong. He also delivers a short sermon to the plants on growing upright and strong.

Vicar of St George

Reverend Clement Hedges has served the local folk for longer than anyone can remember. He certainly can't remember how long he's been there – he's so dotty he doesn't even know what he did last week! Despite his eccentric ways, the vegetable loving parishoners all know that they can come to St George's at any time and hear a good strong sermon on the perils of leaf rot and other gardening-related ills.

Like many churches, the roof of St George's is in need of repair.

St George's

WELCOME TO OUR PARISH CHURCH. Built in 1313, there was some controversy over its name, as members of the Growbag family were worried that a "St George's" church might attract angry dragons on revenge missions. These superstitious ramblings were finally ignored. Since then, there has been talk of a Were-rabbit and zombie snails, which were spotted by Mr Mulch on the way home from cider-tasting club.

A message from our vicar

"Pride is a sin. Should you have any large carrots to be proud of, I suggest you demonstrate humility by NOT showing them at the vegetable competition. Give someone else a chance, like... ahem... me."

The organ fund

Violet Wallflower, our organist, has been having trouble with her arias. We seek cash to fund the search for the dead owl who is stuck in one of the pipes. In return, Violet has agreed to forget her days as the Manglers' keyboard player, and never play heavy metal hits in church again.

Violet also likes playing incidental music from old horror films. We have asked her politely to put a sock in it.

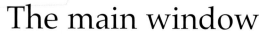

The main window

Featuring St George slaying the dragon, this window was in fact supposed to be just one in a series. The next window was intended to depict St George slicing the dragon up then mincing it into burgers, but this idea made some parishioners feel a bit sick, and it was abandoned.

• The Latin inscription reads "stained glass windows on special offer this week"! Scrawled on the plans, it was included on the window by mistake.

• Some say that the St George myth is simply an exaggeration of Old George Mulch (Mr Mulch's ancestor) having a bit of trouble slicing up a particularly fiery radish.

• Locals believe the holy grail (in the flower-shaped window) is hidden in the Tottington Hall greenhouse, where it is used as a cactus pot.

• If you wish to admire the window today, you're a bit late – it now has a Were-rabbit-shaped hole in it.

• Plans have begun to replace the broken window with a scene of the townsfolk slaying the Were-rabbit.

• A sponsored bunny-hop in memory of the poor beast will be held around the allotments on St Agnes' Eve.

Font

For hundreds of years people have been christened in this font. For a short spell babies were given silly names, but in recent times locals have made a concerted effort to stop this by giving their offspring sensible, vegetable-related names.

Candelabra

With the candles removed, this lovely piece of ornate ironwork comes in very handy at the town fair as a coconut shy.

Harvest of Horror

Decorative bread was ripped to shreds

It was a Harvest Festival Eve much like any other. Reverend Hedges had prepared a basket of carrots to add to the traditional offering table – not his best carrots, of course, but some slightly weedy ones. He had said a little prayer in the hope that his vegetables might grow (bigger and stronger than anyone else's) – but then things took a sinister turn....

Basket of onions never stood a chance

This small display was also wrecked by the power of a monstrous bunny paw. The main vegetable display was decimated.

Grave happenings

A dark figure lumbered towards the church, so huge and ungainly it could only have been Mrs Mulch – but it wasn't! Perhaps the reverend shouldn't have said to the creature "take whatever you like" – the creature took it all.

Banner by Mrs Mulch in ruins

Rabbit-shaped hole in window

Police barrier put up by PC Mackintosh

The monster left the flowers untouched

Vegecidal rage

When the creature lolloped out of the shadows, the vicar saw that he faced the mythical Were-rabbit! Thinking swiftly he created a cross by holding up two handy cucumbers, but they were chomped from his hands – the creature saw them as a tasty entrée! The vicar's cries for mercy grew fainter as he passed out, and the beast set about its feeding frenzy.

Remember in your prayers...

• Miss Blight's potatoes – mashed.
• Mr Caliche's peas – mushy.
• Mr Windfall's pears – halved.
• Lady Tottington's oranges – squashed.

Town Meeting

A night of cauliflower carnage and spinach slaughter drives the local folk to the brink of hysteria. There aren't many things that can get the whole town into church at once. Reverend Hedges' "hear one, get one free" special sermon offer certainly hasn't worked. However, a threat to the townsfolk's vegetables certainly does the trick.

Judgement day

PC Mackintosh thinks the attack is due to rivalry between gardeners. However, the crowd parts and the half-demented Reverend appears, revealing that a creature with ears like tombstones and teeth like axe blades has struck. Because the townsfolk have forced innocent turnips and pure-hearted peas to grow beyond natural size, a dreadful punishment has fallen on them – in the form of the Were-rabbit!

The vicar usually employs his bath chair to run over snails, but also uses it for dramatic entrances.

Ideas to defeat the beast

- Mr Crock suggested using his lopping tool. Many people present were too busy fainting to comment.

- Mr Dibber suggested creating a Were-ferret to hunt it down. But who would catch the Were-ferret?

- Mrs Mulch said disguising a stick of dynamite as a carrot would produce enough bunny bits to create 3,000 Were-pies.

Mr Crock's lopping tool

The terrible truth

The Reverend's news comes as a shock. Eyes pop, mouths hang open and stunned expressions appear on the faces of the locals. Who will be able to save their beloved Giant Vegetable Competition?

Victor to the rescue

Heroes come in all shapes and sizes, but none as odd as towering, toupee-wearing Victor Quartermaine. He only offers to hunt the monster because he thinks the feeble-minded vicar has merely been attacked by a real bunny. He is looking forward to a chance to blow something sweet and furry to bits.

Good versus evil

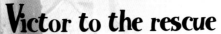

Taking a high moral standpoint, Lady Tottington believes that it is not right to kill any animal that is really rather fluffy. She calls upon Anti-pesto to save the town's produce. Looking at the people around him, Victor comments that there are some vegetables that are beyond saving.

Town saviour

Wallace steps fearlessly forward with his master plan to catch the Were-rabbit – with a big trap! Very soon he might wish he'd kept his big trap shut.

Hunt the Rabbit

They say revenge is a dish best served cold, but, according to Victor, a Were-rabbit could be warmed up as part of a tasty hotpot, or roasted with garlic and served with a salad. Whatever its fate, one thing's certain – no vegetables will sleep soundly in their beds until the buck-toothed beast has been stopped!

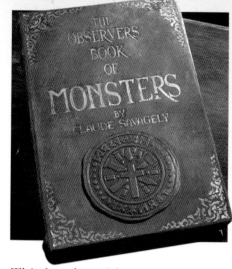

This handy guide to monsters reveals a cunning way to kill the foe – use a golden bullet.

Victor the bunny slayer!

Stopping the monster has even more appeal to Victor now that he knows he'll be shooting Wallace at the same time – a chance to get rid of two big-eared nuisances at once. The reverend gives him the means to do the dark deed – a bullet made of 24 carat gold! Victor is all ears to hear about the beast – if the dramatic lightning outside ever gives him the chance.

Lead us into temptation

It may look like a daft bunny puppet with lipstick and false eyelashes to you, but the model female rabbit built by Wallace is a maddening temptation to a romantic Were-rabbit! To lure the beast, the decoy sits on the van roof and is operated by Gromit via strings attached to his wrists and ankles. The only flaw in their plan is the low bridge ahead of them. The decoy works and Gromit manages to lasso the beast, but finds himself (and the van) dragged into a giant-size burrow!

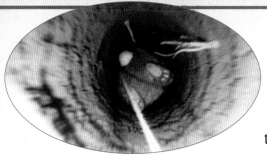

From whence it came...

When the Were-rabbit emerges, Gromit pursues it through countless gardens and underground in the van until the monster reaches its lair.

Caught the culprit

Gromit is in for rather a surprise when the Were-rabbit's tracks lead back to his own home! Gromit thinks there can only be one culprit. In times of crisis, innocent souls sometimes get sucked into the vortex of peril. Hutch, once an ordinary rabbit, is now accused of being a monster.

Giant pawprints that lead up the stairs to Wallace's room tell a startled Gromit that something is afoot – perhaps he was wrong...

The Were-rabbit

Quiver! Quake! Quail! Especially if you're a root vegetable. Was it the result of sharing brainwaves with a bunny in the Mind-o-matic or being forced to stick to a diet of crunchy vegetables that tipped Wallace over the edge? Whatever the cause, Wallace is transformed into a carrot-demolishing engine of destruction with the burrowing power of a London Underground Tunnel-Extending Machine!

Strong arms help Were-rabbit pull vegetables from their beds

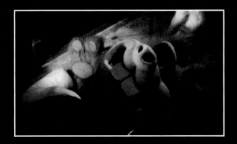

Transformation

Wallace's hands turn into paws, his nostrils flare and his middle-teeth jut horrifyingly downwards. After a monstrous furry makeover, the mutation is finally complete when a cute tail appears on his bottom. As a Were-rabbit he has a fiendish hunger and immense super-bunny strength. Yet, a tiny spark of humanity survives deep in his nibbling-obsessed brain.

The were-withal

• The Were-rabbit's latin name is *Carrotus apetitus giganticus.*

• The bunny beast is a protected species in certain countries.

• The Transylvanians tried to enter a Were-rabbit in the 1972 Olympics but were unable to get the event moved to coincide with a full moon.

• Do not wear a lucky rabbit's foot to ward off a Were-rabbit. It just annoys them.

• Boffins estimate that a Were-rabbit is more fluffy than 13,042 sweet kittens put together. But a Were-rabbit is a lot scarier!

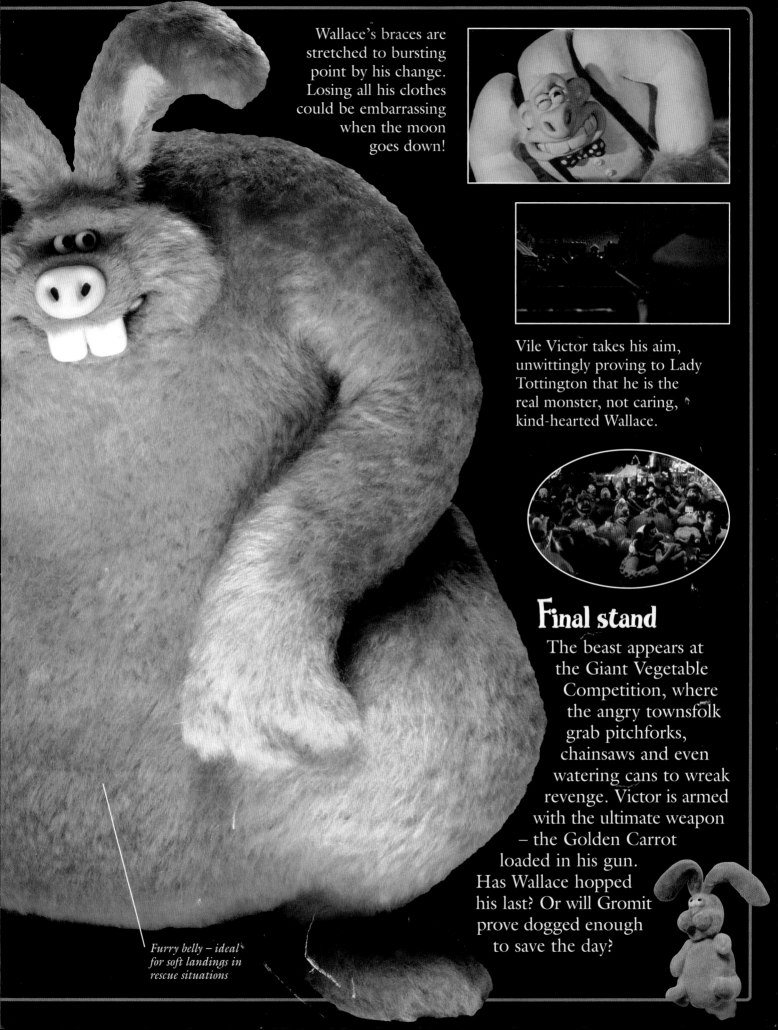

Wallace's braces are stretched to bursting point by his change. Losing all his clothes could be embarrassing when the moon goes down!

Vile Victor takes his aim, unwittingly proving to Lady Tottington that he is the real monster, not caring, kind-hearted Wallace.

Final stand

The beast appears at the Giant Vegetable Competition, where the angry townsfolk grab pitchforks, chainsaws and even watering cans to wreak revenge. Victor is armed with the ultimate weapon – the Golden Carrot loaded in his gun. Has Wallace hopped his last? Or will Gromit prove dogged enough to save the day?

Furry belly – ideal for soft landings in rescue situations

LONDON, NEW YORK, MUNICH,
MELBOURNE, AND DELHI

SENIOR ART EDITOR Guy Harvey   **PROJECT EDITOR** Lindsay Fernandes

ART DIRECTOR Mark Richards   **PUBLISHING MANAGER** Simon Beecroft

DTP DESIGNER Lauren Egan   **CATEGORY PUBLISHER** Alex Kirkham

PRODUCTION Claire Pearson

First Published in Great Britain in 2005 by
Dorling Kindersley Limited
80 Strand, London WC2R 0RL
A Penguin Company

05 06 07 08 09 10 9 8 7 6 5 4 3 2 1

A CIP catalogue record for this book is
available from the British Library.

ISBN 1-4053-1019-7

Reproduced by Colour Systems, U.K.
Printed and bound by Leefung, China.

Acknowledgments
DK Publishing would like to thank:
Rachael Carpenter, Helen Neno,
Yalda Armian, Angie Last and all
the staff at Aardman; thanks also to
Laura Gilbert for proof reading
and editorial assistance.

Discover more at
www.dk.com